NORTHAMPTON
IN
50
BUILDINGS

LORNA TALBOTT

AMBERLEY

First published 2020

Amberley Publishing, The Hill, Stroud
Gloucestershire GL5 4EP

www.amberley-books.com

British Library Cataloguing in Publication Data.
A catalogue record for this book is available from the British Library.

ISBN 978 1 4456 9513 6 (print)
ISBN 978 1 4456 9514 3 (ebook)

Typesetting by Aura Technology and Software Services, India.
Printed in Great Britain.

Contents

Map   4

Key   6

Introduction   7

The 50 Buildings   10

Bibliography   96

Key

1. Northampton Castle
2. Church of the Holy Sepulchre
3. St Peter's Church
4. St John's Church and Hall
5. Delaprè Abbey
6. Quinton House School
7. Abington Park, Abbey and Pigeon Tower
8. Hazelrigg House
9. The Welsh House
10. Old Black Lion
11. Sessions House
12. No. 18 Market Square
13. All Saints Church
14. United Reformed Church
15. Northampton and County Club
16. General Hospital
17. Gibraltar Barracks
18. The Corporation Charity School
19. Northampton Cathedral
20. St Andrew's Hospital
21. St Thomas à Becket's Well
22. County Hall
23. The Parade (former Corn Exchange)
24. Clare Street Drill Hall
25. Beckett and Sargeant's School
26. College Street Chapel
27. Guildhall
28. No. 1 Victoria Gardens
29. Crockett and Jones Shoe Factory
30. Albion Brewery
31. Museum and Art Gallery
32. Royal and Derngate Theatre
33. The Bear
34. St Matthew's Church
35. City Building
36. Central Library
37. Northampton School for Boys
38. Barratts Shoe Factory
39. No. 78 Derngate
40. Memorial Hall
41. New Ways
42. Racecourse Pavilion
43. The Jesus Centre
44. Mounts Baths
45. Abington Library
46. Carlsberg Brewery
47. International Academy
48. The National Lift Tower
49. *Discovery* (the Francis Crick Memorial)
50. Northgate Bus Station

Introduction

Northampton nestles quietly in the very centre of England. It is the county town of Northamptonshire, but despite the presence of a cathedral, it has never been granted city status. Northampton, however, has the prestige of being the largest town in the country. *Northampton in 50 Buildings* explores the fascinating history of this Midlands town through some of its wonderful architecture.

Northampton originated in the Bronze Age over 3,000 years ago. At this time, the first settlers utilised the fertile land by the river as an area for encampments. Later, Iron Age people moved to the high ground of the nearby hills to settle, where the good visibility provided safety from other tribes. There is some evidence of occupation in the area during Roman times, but it was the invasion of the Danes in the ninth century that heralded the beginning of the town of Northampton. The Guildhall commemorates the influence of the Danes in a frieze situated just inside the building.

It was from the Danes that Northampton gained its name. In 914 the town of 'Ham Tune' is first recorded in writing, which is Danish and translates to 'home town'. When the Domesday Book was written in 1086, the prefix of North had been added to differentiate it from similarly named towns such as 'South Ham

Northampton has some wonderful buildings displaying differing architectural styles.

Tune'. By the thirteenth century the town's spelling was identical to its current one, making it one of the oldest original spellings of a place name in the country.

The Norman Conquest, and the subsequent appointment of Norman noblemen as the Earls of Northampton, meant that the town began to grow. The castle was built and this became an important stronghold in the Norman landscape. Northampton's was an important castle due to its strategic position in the centre of the country and it became the seat of parliament and a royal residence. There were many impressive churches built at this time, including the unique, round Church of the Holy Sepulchre. It was during the early years of William the Conqueror's reign as monarch of England that the town was first enclosed behind strong protective walls.

Northampton street names reveal how the town created a living during medieval times. Both Mercer Row and Sheep Street provide evidence that Northampton used to be an important wool town, but when the livestock subsequently changed to mainly cattle, this, with the proximity of the River Nene, led to the rise of the tanning and shoemaking industry. Northampton is known as the shoe capital of England and many architecturally impressive tanneries and shoe factories remain from the nineteenth century.

Northampton castle disappeared in an act of retribution by Royalist troops after Northampton sided with the supporters of Oliver Cromwell during the English Civil War. They pulled the castle down and shortly afterwards another devastating loss of ancient property occurred. In 1675 Northampton suffered an enormous fire that swept through the town. There are a few buildings that predate the fire and survive only because they are stone built – the timber buildings were all destroyed. Subsequently, Northampton essentially became a 'New Town'. Following the fire, it was necessary to rebuild and important seventeenth-century architectural works were produced.

The ancient Church of the Holy Sepulchre is fascinating.

The term 'New Town' occurred again to denote Northampton in the twentieth century. Following the Second World War, in 1948, there was an official wave of new towns. These were designed to accommodate the vast number of people, especially from bombed-out inner cities, who had been displaced by the war. Northampton was a designated 'new town' but building was gradual and by the time Northampton began to build its vast new housing estates, it was the 1960s. The locality to the M1 motorway and other transport links meant that Northampton's expansion was used as part of the northward-creeping commuter belt of London. The mass influx of new residents created a need for more shops to cater for them, and the Grosvenor Centre in the heart of the town was one of the first shopping malls in the country. It is built in 1970s brutalist style and this type of architecture is also exhibited by a main employer of the town, Carlsberg, whose brewery is an award-winning piece of design.

The changing fortunes of Northampton over the last 1,000 years has produced a wealth of interesting buildings with a wide diversity of styles. These range from the fragments of the Norman castle through to the National Lift Tower, a modern building that dominates the skyline for miles around. The architecture is imposing, and encompasses important churches, beautiful examples of industrial buildings, civic masterpieces, cosy pubs and nationally important properties like the house designed by Rennie Mackintosh on Derngate. This look at Northampton through fifty buildings offers the reader the opportunity to discover the treasures of this Midlands town and its fascinating history.

The Carlsberg brewery has a riverside setting.

The 50 Buildings

1. Northampton Castle (1084)

All that remains of Northampton Castle are a few fragments. However, for over 500 years after its construction in the eleventh century, it was one of the most important Norman castles in the country. It was built by Simon de Senlis as a fortified dwelling in 1084. Northampton was the first large castle reached after leaving London and it became a favourite place for the king to visit and enjoy the hunting and jousting hosted there. The castle was so favoured that it became the seat of parliament during medieval times and many trials, including that of Thomas Becket, were held within its walls.

The Black Death in the fourteenth century devastated society and afterwards the castle was used less by the king and parliament. Northampton was a Roundhead stronghold during the English Civil War in the seventeenth century, and they used the castle as defence from troops loyal to the crown. Charles II was eventually

Northampton Castle was favoured in medieval England.

victorious and ordered that the castle be demolished in retribution for the people of Northampton siding with the Roundheads.

Only one bastion tower was left and was used as the county jail. The rest of the sandstone blocks that had been used in the castle building were taken away from the site and reused to build various properties around the town. The foundations could still be seen in Victorian times but these were finally removed when the railway came to Northampton in the nineteenth century and the castle site was used to build the railway station.

Northampton castle would have been a magnificent structure. It commanded a large site, protected on three sides by deep trenches and on the other side by a branch of the river Nene. It had an imposing keep and very high defensive walls. The castle mound can still be seen near the railway. When the railway station was re-built in the 1960s, the site was excavated and the many finds are now on display in the museum.

The only other remaining part of the castle is a postern gate, which can be seen from the main road near the railway station. A postern gate was a smaller doorway in the defensive walls of a castle that, due to their size, were both easy to defend and a safer means of escape. The postern arch is now set into a wall rebuilt with some of the original castle stone.

Below left: Northampton Castle's site can be seen near the railway station.

Below right: The only remnant of the castle is the postern gate.

2. Church of the Holy Sepulchre (1100)

The Church of the Holy Sepulchre, on Sheep Street, is a very rare example of a round-built church. It is of national historical importance and is Grade I listed. The order for its building and consecration was made by Simon de Senlis, the first Norman Earl of Northampton, in 1100. The church is now the oldest building still standing in Northampton.

Simon de Senlis took part in the first crusade to the Holy Land in 1096. He travelled to Jerusalem, and here he saw the Church of the Holy Sepulchre, which marks the birthplace of Christ. He was so inspired by this magnificent piece of architecture, which is still standing in Jerusalem, that on his return to Northampton he had a replica built. The Northampton church was half the size of the one in the Holy City but no less as impressive. It was originally called the Crusader Round before changing its name to reflect the original.

The church has had many alterations over the years, and the fact that the church was originally round is not immediately obvious from the outside. There has been a nave, chancel, transepts and porches added, all completely altering the exterior. However, on entering the church the original round construction is unmistakeable, with the eight Norman piers surrounding the circular area that is now the baptistry.

The Church of the Holy Sepulchre dates from 1100.

The interior of the Church of the Holy Sepulchre.

The latest alterations were done in the nineteenth century by Sir George Gilbert Scott, who added a chancel screen that had been created by his son, Oldrid, and stained-glass windows by the William Morris studio. The Victorians had an interest in medieval church design, and particularly the use of wall paintings. Medieval paintings added colour to church walls in the years before the Reformation, after which they were whitewashed over and became plain. Where possible, Victorian church restorers tried to uncover the original wall paintings that were often hidden below many layers of whitewash. The Church of the Holy Sepulchre had none of its original painting remaining, but Scott used new paint schemes to add colour to the roof beams and the top of the window arches. This complements the history and heritage of the ancient ironstone church.

The Church of the Holy Sepulchre's porch has a round wall.

3. St Peter's Church (1130)

This outstanding Norman church, situated on Marefair, is dedicated to St Peter. It was constructed during the major remodelling of Northampton by Simon de Senlis in the years following the Norman Conquest and replaced an earlier Saxon place of worship. A ninth-century grave slab inside the church, with intricate stone designs, is from the earlier church.

More stunning carving can be seen inside St Peter's on the capitals that decorate the pillars. These depict foliage, birds and animals and also feature some curious human faces. Although carved in the eleventh century, for many years the capitals were not on show as they had been plastered over in the seventeenth century. It was only due to the dedication of a Victorian historian, who singlehandedly uncovered them over the course of eleven years, that these lost decorations can now be seen.

The Grade I listed Church of St Peter is built of both ironstone, which has a reddish hue, and limestone, which is pale in appearance. These two construction mediums are combined throughout the building to great decorative effect and complement the exterior tiers of arcades. The niches would have originally contained statuary but these were removed and destroyed in the sixteenth century.

St Peter's is an attractive Norman church.

Intricate carving
over St Peter's
west window.

The arched Norman windows and doorways date from the twelfth century as does a magnificent decorative stone arch above the west window.

St Peter's was restored in the mid-nineteenth century by Sir George Gilbert Scott, who added stained glass and interior woodwork in the Victorian style. Scott also preserved the remaining Norman features and fourteenth-century font. There is an elaborate stencil design on the interior east wall completed by Scott's son, John. Another Victorian feature is a bust to William Smith, an eminent Victorian scientist dubbed the 'father of geology', who died locally and is buried in the churchyard.

Despite its history St Peter's dwindling congregation caused it to close in 1995. However, the dedication of The Friends of St Peter's has ensured it has been passed to the Church Conservation Trust, who have since looked after it. The trust found interior damage was being caused by a mould growing on impermeable oil paint applied during the Victorian restoration. This all had to be removed and replaced with something breathable.

The church is now sound again and, as an important Norman building, has become a visitor attraction, and it still holds occasional services. The 'friends' promote the church as a local venue and it has continued to be an important part of the community.

4. St John's Church and Hall (1138)

Now the oldest secular buildings still standing in Northampton, these two adjoining properties were originally consecrated and used by a monastic order to care for the sick.

The church and hall are both Grade I listed and stand on Bridge Street. St John's church was the chapel for St John's Hospital, and the hall was the infirmary.

St John's was part of a medieval hospital complex.

When it was founded in 1138, the purpose of a hospital was slightly different. Run by monks, it sheltered the poor or needy, took in orphans and also offered accommodation to those on pilgrimage. There was an infirmary where the monks cared for those residents who were ill.

In the twentieth century an archaeological excavation of an adjacent site was completed. It revealed the medieval rubbish pits that were used by the hospital. The contents of these give an insight into the lifestyle of the monks who ran it. The hospital received funds from both the Crown and charitable donations and they lived well. The quantity of sheep and cow bones indicated that they ate a meat-rich diet and they ate cherries, plums and figs, which commanded a high price. Bones found in the pits from mink and ermine displayed damage indicative of skinning and tanning and provide evidence that the Fathers of St John showed off their wealth by wearing fur.

Both of the buildings that remain from the original hospital complex are built of stone and have slate roofs. The interiors have their original oak ceiling beams and the west wall of St John's hall has a tall, arched doorway that reaches up to a fourteenth-century traceried window. The former chapel building has also retained its original windows.

The hospital ceased to be used when Henry VIII ordered the Dissolution of the Monasteries. After the Reformation, the hall was used as an almshouse, and from 1955 to 1990 the chapel was reconsecrated and used as the Roman Catholic Church of St John. The site was eventually bought by developers and became 'The Church', a restaurant and bar offering hospitality to all, echoing the original hospital of 900 years ago.

St John's hall
has windows
dating from
the fourteenth
century.

5. Delaprè Abbey (1145)

In 1145, just outside the town walls of Northampton, the Norman Earl of
Northampton, Simon de Senlis, gave land to a group of nuns from the Cluniac
order to build a nunnery. They named it the Abbey of St Mary de la Prè, meaning
'St Mary in the meadow'. Over time its title has been corrupted to become
Delaprè Abbey.

When the much-loved wife of Edward I died at Lincoln in 1291, her body
was taken to London to be interred. On the journey to Westminster Abbey, the
cortège rested at Delaprè Abbey Church. Edward later decreed that a stone
cross be erected at each stop that his beloved wife's body had made on her final
journey and one was built at Delaprè. The octagonal cross still stands and is an
impressive structure, with fine stone statues around it. It was restored by the
Victorians but is largely unaltered. Its Grade I listing as an ancient monument
reflects its intact state.

In 1460 another major event affected the nuns at the abbey. The Battle of
Northampton, a major battle of the Wars of the Roses, took place on the abbey
meadow. The engagement resulted in Henry VI being defeated and he was kept
prisoner in the abbey on the night of his capture. The nuns also tended the wounds
of the injured on the battlefield, and many of the dead were buried in the nun's
graveyard. This has now become the site of the walled garden.

After 400 years, in the reign of Henry VIII, the abbey disappeared. In 1538,
during the Dissolution of the Monasteries, Henry evicted the nuns and took all
of their lands and possessions for himself. The abbey and grounds were bought
by the Tate family, who went on to build the property that can be seen on the

Left: An Eleanor cross is sited near Delaprè Abbey.

Below: The house where Delaprè Abbey stood is of Tudor origin.

Delaprè Abbey has a magnificent interior.

site today. The only remaining echo of the original abbey is the central courtyard, which follows the layout of the abbey cloisters.

When the final owner of Delaprè Abbey died in 1943, the house was passed on to the ownership of Northampton council. Due to the poor state of repair of the fine neoclassical house, there were plans to demolish it, but fortunately campaigners saved the property and the building was used as the Northamptonshire Records Office. The grounds were opened up as public parkland.

By the twenty-first century the house was considered 'at risk' despite its Grade II listed status; the Records Office had moved out and the stone-built property was falling into disrepair. A Heritage Lottery Fund grant was secured to save the house and it is now in the process of restoration. A lot of architectural work has been completed and some of the house, with its battlemented parapet, clock tower and impressive crenelated entrance porch is available to hire as a wedding venue. Other rooms in the abbey, its gardens and parkland are open to the public. As more funds are raised, more of Delaprè Abbey will be restored to its former glory and opened to all.

6. Quinton House School (1419)

Quinton House Boarding School is just off the main Weedon Road. The school building and adjacent St Michael's Church are the remains of the deserted village of Upton and have a long history. The school has occupied the site since 1946 when Upton Hall was leased by three female members of the Teape family. It was in a state of disrepair but the ladies restored it and opened it as a school for girls.

Upton Hall is a Grade I listed property and has original features from 1419, when the Knightley family built the manor house on becoming lords of the village of Upton. They created a three-storey red-brick house with stone windows. The hall was rebuilt by Thomas Samwell in the late fifteenth century and the façade and door facings are from this date. The west wing was added a few years later to create an 'L'-shaped building and further redevelopments occurred at the end of the eighteenth century. The four round-arched niches by the entrance porch were added at this time and contain statues of the four seasons.

The interior has a magnificent two-storey great hall and the roof beams from the original 1419 property can be seen in the roof space above the plaster ceiling. Quinton House has large, grand rooms, and the ballroom, which dates from the 1730s, has excellent examples of plaster work reliefs. This stucco work was done by Guiseppe Artari and Giovanni Bagutti, who were the leaders in their field at that time.

The garden contains a round, wrought-iron aviary resting on a brick base. It dates from the beginning of the Victorian era and has a Grade II listing. The garden also contains a fourteenth-century Gothic arch, which is believed to have been removed from the neighbouring St Michael's Church.

Fifteenth-century Upton Hall is now Quinton House School.

Above: There has been worship at St Michael's since Saxon times.

Below: St Michael's churchyard has a gravestone with listed status.

St Michael's Church is Grade I listed and has Norman origins. Worship on the site occurred earlier, however. An excavation in the churchyard revealed a seventh-century Saxon timber structure that may have been a church for the villagers of Upton. The graveyard contains a rare, Grade II listed tombstone from the seventeenth century and also the base of a medieval cross.

Upton village disappeared long ago. Some traces of the lost village remain near Quinton House. Fishponds and wells can be determined through markings in the grass and the fields still bear the signs of ridge and furrow farming methods. Upton, like many other villages, was deserted in medieval times, when the Black Death wiped out most of the population. The few survivors moved away and the village gradually disappeared, leaving only the manor house and church.

7. Abington Park, Abbey and Pigeon Tower (1530)

The village of Abington was recorded in the Domesday Book of 1086. It continued to thrive throughout medieval times, until the land was enclosed and depopulated in the seventeenth century. The eviction was to provide parkland for the Thursby family, who had taken ownership of the Abington estate. All that now remains of the village is the manor house, the Church of St Peter and St Paul and a few fragments of wall.

One of the remains from the ancient village of Abington.

Behind the Georgian façade, Abington Abbey has sixteenth-century features.

Abington manor house, later known as Abington Abbey despite no ecclesiastical link, is a Grade I listed building dating from the sixteenth century. It became the marital home of Elizabeth, the granddaughter of William Shakespeare, who is buried in the nearby twelfth-century Church of St Peter and St Paul. When the Thursby family took over Abington, they remodelled the manor house completely. Only the Oak Room, with wooden panelled walls, still retains its original appearance. The stone front of the building now has a Georgian façade, with the simple classical styling of Doric pilasters dating from a rebuild of 1740. The building was briefly used as an asylum in the mid-nineteenth century, after the Thursby family left. This has led to a reputation as a haunted house.

Abington Park's other notable structure is the pigeon tower. This stone structure was built on the order of William Thursby when he changed the village to parkland in 1678. The tower had two uses: the upper storey is a pigeon coop and the lower storey contains a well and pump. The pigeons would have provided meat for the family and the well would have been used to provide water for other livestock in the park. The pigeon tower has a Grade II listing and is an eye-catching feature of the area.

Abington is still a park. It was given in its entirety to the people of Northampton in 1897. The manor is now the site of a museum and the park has gradually become more recreational as boating lakes, an aviary, bandstands and children's play equipment have been added over the years.

The pigeon tower in Abington Park is a picturesque sight.

8. Hazelrigg House (1562)

Hazelrigg House, on Marefair, is commonly known as Cromwell House due to its link with Oliver Cromwell. Northampton was loyal to the Roundheads and their commonwealth cause during the English Civil War of the 1640s, and their commander, Oliver Cromwell, stayed in the town on his way to the Battle of Naseby in 1645. It was Hazelrigg House where he reputedly spent the night and as it was one of the few stone buildings in Northampton at that time, the house would certainly have been a prestigious enough property to offer him a bed.

The property survived the 1675 fire that ravaged through the wooden buildings of the town; however, despite its stone walls and slate roof, Hazelrigg House was still badly damaged. The property originally had five dormers when it was built in 1562, but now has only three. Fire damage reduced the width of the house dramatically. The surviving gable ends of the dormers are typical of Elizabethan design, as are the diamond latticed, mullioned windows, but none of the original features survive inside. The building is an important piece of Northampton history and has a Grade II listing.

The house gets its current name from the family who owned it for nearly 300 years. The Hazelrigg family were rich Northampton landlords. They owned a lot

Sixteenth-century Hazelrigg House has links to Oliver Cromwell.

of property in the town centre, and, after the castle was pulled down by Royalists following the Civil War, the family bought the castle site, although they never developed it. This only occurred when they sold the land to the railways in the nineteenth century and the castle area became the railway station.

9. The Welsh House (1595)

The Welsh House is an important Grade II listed building on Northampton's Market Square. It adjoins the Grosvenor Shopping Centre and whilst it contrasts completely with the mall's modern appearance, this serves to highlight the sixteenth century survivor of Northampton's Great Fire.

The fire that devastated Northampton began on 20 September 1675, and within six hours, three quarters of the town had been destroyed. Seven hundred families lost their homes, but the Welsh House is the reason why only eleven people lost their lives. As the flames raged through every one of the wooden buildings surrounding the central market, the stone-built Welsh House did not catch fire. Residents used it as an escape route from the Market Square and certain death as the fire closed in from all sides.

Left: The ancient Welsh House is now among modern buildings.

Below: The Welsh House provided an escape from the burning market.

The Welsh House is named after its Celtic motto.

The blaze had been started by a stray spark from an open fire in a cottage situated near the castle. The flames soon engulfed it and a strong westerly wind drove the fire through the tightly packed streets of wooden thatched properties. Every house in central Northampton that was not stone built burned. After the fire, residents and local businesses raised money to rebuild the town. With the help of a generous donation from the king, the reconstruction was completed very quickly. The new Northampton properties were built of stone and slate, standing on widened streets to ensure a similar tragedy did not occur.

The Welsh House has the same appearance as at the time of the fire, although it is now being used as a modern restaurant and bar. It is built of a mellow coloured stone and has a slate roof. Set into this are dormer windows with decorative shaping and finials. The house also has original mullioned casement windows. The building dates from 1595 and gets the name 'Welsh House' from the stone inscription it bears. This says 'Heb Dyw/Heb Dym/Dwya/Digon', which translates to 'Without God/ Without Everything/ With God/ Enough'. This motto has been the source of contemplation for many of the residents of Northampton for over four centuries.

10. Old Black Lion (1675)

The Old Black Lion Inn is named after the street on which it stands, Black Lion Hill. It was built in 1675 and stands by the ancient Church of St Peter. It is a Grade II listed building.

Northampton supported the Parliamentarians during the civil war of the 1640s, and afterwards the Royalists decided to demolish Northampton Castle to penalise the town for allying themselves with Oliver Cromwell. The original Norman stone blocks of the castle were reused to build other properties. The Black Lion Inn was one of them. Originally built as The Plasterers Arms, the inn is designed to be homely with its buttery stone walls, steep Welsh slate roof and tall, narrow chimneys.

The name was changed to The Old Black Lion in 1720 and since then the inn has gained notoriety for being haunted. Over the years, people have reported hearing footsteps and voices coming from empty corridors and rooms, and a few shocked customers have heard a woman's screams and a baby crying.

In 1892, the then proprietor, Andrew McRae, brutally murdered his lover and their child in the bar. He dismembered the bodies, put them in a suitcase and hid it below a platform at the nearby railway station. MacRae had failed to realise that his name was inside the suitcase and, when the remains were found, he was soon arrested for the crime. He became the last murderer to be hanged in Northampton in 1893. The spooky noises are supposedly the dying screams of his lover, Anne Pritchard, and their baby's cries can be heard as it witnesses the event.

The Old Black Lion Inn contains the demolished castle's masonry.

11. Sessions House (1676)

Northampton's Sessions House is considered to be the finest local courthouse in the country and has been given a Grade I listing to acknowledge this fact. The ironstone building is on George Row and it was the first property to be completed in the rebuild of Northampton following the devastating fire of 1675.

Notable architect Henry Bell was responsible for its design and construction in 1676, and his trademark baroque design features can be seen throughout. The building has classical styling with Corinthian pilasters complementing the tall arched doorways, and the doors themselves have swag relief detailing. The Sessions House has a decorative stone balustrade around a Welsh slate roof. The property used to have a cupola but this was removed when it was considered too expensive to repair. The interior of the property has plasterwork ceilings of an exceptionally high standard from the seventeenth century.

The Sessions House was used to hold county assizes for nearly 300 years, until the court moved in 1993. The building is now used as a tourist information office. The original cells can be seen in the basement and in 1705 these were the final home of the last two women to be tried for witchcraft in England. They were

Northampton's Sessions House is an exceptional seventeenth-century building.

The Sessions House held trials for over 300 years.

found guilty in the Northampton court and later hanged. The unreliable methods used in trials of witchcraft were put into question soon after this trial and the death penalty for witchcraft was subsequently abolished.

12. No. 18 Market Square (1676)

No. 18 Market Square is an attractive, blue painted town house on the south side of the market. Its exterior appearance is much the same as when the property was originally built, just after the great fire of Northampton, in 1676. Any alterations have been on the ground floor where it has been adapted for trading and has had shop windows added. Original internal features, including fireplaces and roof beams, remain and the historical importance of the building has won it a Grade II listing.

The three-storey property was built in brick and covered with painted stucco. It has attractive Ionic pilasters and elegant swag details. These are synonymous with the renowned seventeenth-century architect Henry Bell, and he is believed to have designed No. 18.

Northampton Market Square is one of the largest in Europe and Northampton market has always been one of the most important in the country. The original market charter was granted in 1189 for the people of Northampton to hold a market in the grounds of All Saints Church. However, trading and bartering was banned on church land in 1235 and the market moved to the site that it still occupies, nearly 800 years later.

The square was paved in the sixteenth century and held four major horse markets each year. All local produce was traded there and it was the site for other entertainments and attractions. In 1828 a hot air balloon attempted to take off from the square but it could not gain enough elevation. The balloon was too high to be retethered and the pilot could not climb down. As the balloon approached

No. 18 Market Square has brightly painted plasterwork detailing.

the buildings surrounding the square, the pilot jumped out into the attic window of No. 18 to escape. The balloon started a panic in the Market Square before eventually being brought under control.

13. All Saints Church (1680)

All Saints Church dominates the central area of Northampton. It has a Grade I listing as a historic church and is a popular meeting point for locals.

It is regularly visited by American tourists who are interested in the history of their country. The Ball family were parishioners of All Saints and emigrated to the Americas in the seventeenth century. A first-generation descendant, Mary, was to become the mother of George Washington, the first President of the United States.

There has been a church on the site since the time of the first Norman lords, when, in the eleventh century, Simon de Senlis built All Hallows Church. This was lost to Northampton's great fire in 1675, but rebuilt and consecrated as All Saints in 1680. After the fire, only the central tower, crypt and part of the font remained. The tower was later rebuilt but the font survives, and the inscription of the sculptor can be seen on it. The font is Anglo-Saxon and was removed from an earlier church on the same site.

After the great fire, the king donated most of the money for the rebuilding of the town despite Northampton's allegiance to Cromwell during the Civil War. Much of this donation went to the reconstruction of the church. There is a statue of Charles II, erected in thanks to him, on the portico at the front of All Saints.

The architect responsible for the church was Henry Bell, a contemporary of Christopher Wren. This connection is strikingly evident in the interior of All Saints. The barrel-vaulted nave with fine, delicate plasterwork and a central dome, supported on four Ionic columns, is reminiscent of St Paul's cathedral in London. The dome allows natural light to enter the church through its high windows, while other lighting is supplied by elaborate chandeliers. The focal point in the aisle is the gilded altar piece.

Externally, there are two contrasting colours of stonework used to good decorative effect. A balustrade highlights the wide portico, which rests on Doric columns, and incorporates the figure of the king. The church was designed to be square and has a central tower that is topped with a copper cupola and weathervane.

All Saints Church contains a wealth of history.

The portico of All Saints has popular places to meet.

All Saints Church has a lofty central tower.

14. United Reformed Church (1695)

The United Reformed Church on Doddridge Street was built in 1695. The license to worship on the site was finally granted to the nonconformists in 1672 and the church was built soon afterwards. It was known at that time as the Castle Hill Independent Church and constructed using the reclaimed sandstone blocks that had originally formed part of nearby Northampton castle.

This simply styled church, with a hipped slate roof, has an incredibly accurate sundial set into the front elevation of the same date. The interior has original wooden box pews and galleries and also houses a memorial to Philip Doddridge, the renowned Northampton preacher and philanthropist who gave his name to the street on which the church stands. The memorial is by John Hunt, an apprentice to Grinling Gibbons, and was erected after Doddridge's death in 1751.

Above: The United Reformed Church has a simple but stylish design.

Left: The United Reformed Church has an accurate seventeenth-century sundial.

15. Northampton and County Club (c. 1700)

The Northampton and County Club is an important piece of architecture in Northampton as it was the first private house built in the reconstruction of Northampton following the devastating fire of 1675.

The building is Grade II listed and occupies a position on George Row. It is built of local stone and has an elegant cream, stuccoed façade with a central porch flanked by Doric columns. The interior boasts an original seventeenth-century staircase and there are fine plasterwork ceilings in the reception rooms, dating from the 1740s.

The modest width of the building's front belies the size of the property beyond. Major alterations occurred in the nineteenth century, when it was adapted to become a gentleman's club. A large extension was added at the rear to house the club's kitchen, dining and bar area and a games room that could fit three full-size billiard tables.

In the basement are elaborate vaulted cellars that date back to the fourteenth century. Although at the time the site was occupied by an inn called the Adam and Eve, it is unlikely that such a well-built cellar was used to store beer. It is more likely that this undercroft was actually another alehouse competing for trade with the Adam and Eve that stood above it.

The club building was a private home for many years and briefly served as the Northampton infirmary during the eighteenth century, before the new general

The small stylish entrance to the Northampton and County Club.

hospital was built. The building went up for sale and was bought by the founders of the Northampton and County Club, who wanted to provide smart premises where gentlemen could 'enjoy chess, billiards and news'. The successful private club now enjoys a mixed membership and is nearly 150 years old. It remains one of the most prestigious venues in Northampton.

16. General Hospital (1793)

Northampton General Hospital occupies a large site on the corner of Billing Road and Cliftonville. It has gradually grown over the years and now has different blocks and wings in a range of architectural styles. The earliest part of the hospital fronts onto Billing Road and was built in 1793. Building has continued into the twenty-first century, with the nurse's accommodation at the rear of the site being the latest addition.

In 1744, local doctor James Stonhouse, together with Northampton philanthropist Philip Doddridge, set out to create the proper hospital that the town desperately needed. They provided enough money to equip a house on George Row for the purpose and this became one of the first voluntarily funded hospitals in Great Britain.

The earliest part of the General Hospital is classically designed.

There are art deco details on the Barratt Maternity Hospital.

By 1793 it became apparent that the George Row site was not large enough and funds were raised for the provision of a better facility. A site was located on Billing Road and a new ninety-five-bed hospital was designed and built by architect Samuel Saxon. This original Georgian building has been Grade II listed for its historical importance. It is built in stone with a Welsh slate roof and stands three storeys high. The classical style includes Doric pilasters and porch columns typical of the period.

Later extensions to the hospital were funded by local shoe manufacturers and one of these is the Barratt maternity home. The maternity building was opened in 1936 and is a good example of art deco architecture. It has a flat roof contemporary to the era and is built in red brick. The art deco railings below the first-floor windows match the metalwork in the door glass, all of which are original. A lovely feature is the pair of storks on either side of the entrance.

During the First World War the hospital provided medical help for over 3,000 wounded soldiers. They did this by filling the grounds with temporary wooden structures, which they used as extra wards. Most of this space is now filled with permanent buildings and car parks.

17. Gibraltar Barracks (1797)

France had a social revolution in 1789, and in its aftermath, there were fears in Westminster that a similar insurrection could occur on British soil. In response to the possible threat of uprising, new barracks buildings were built throughout England to serve two purposes. One aim was to remind any possible dissenters that the armed forces were ever present, and another intention was to stir up a feeling of national pride with a more public display of military ceremony.

Above: Gibraltar Barracks was built for a regiment of military heroes.

Below: The schoolhouse from Gibraltar Barracks is still in use.

Part of the barracks wall survives along Barracks Road.

Gibraltar Barracks was one of these. It was the base for the 58th Regiment of Foot, who named it in honour of their heroic struggle during the Great Siege of Gibraltar, where the 58th Regiment held on to British territory for four years. They held out tirelessly despite being besieged and completely blockaded by the French and Spanish navies during the eighteenth-century conflict.

It had three blocks for accommodation, a large parade ground and a schoolhouse. The barracks were in continual use until 1959 when they became an army pay office. The site was eventually sold to the Royal Mail and the barracks were demolished to create the building that now houses the Northampton International Academy. Army cadets, however, still use a building that stands on an adjacent site.

Some remains of the old barracks survive and the schoolhouse still stands on Barracks Road. It is stone built with a deep pitched slate roof. The traceried windows give the building an ecclesiastical appearance and the large upper floor window and three ground level ones each have an elegant arched design. A fragment of red-brick wall from the original barracks also exists. It contains a stone gateway with a wrought-iron gate, and part of an original stone pilaster with Georgian classical decoration can be seen.

18. The Corporation Charity School (1811)

The Corporation Charity School was built in 1811 on Bridge Street. It has a red-brick construction in the main, but local stone has been used to good decorative effect. The upper floor has an alternating pattern of sash windows interspersed with stone statue niches. The two lower windows were altered in the early twentieth century, when the property was adapted to become commercial premises, but the

The Corporation Charity School has changed little in two centuries.

Grade II listed school building still retains its Georgian appearance. The central doorway and moulded cornice are original, as is the plaque above it bearing the inscription 'The Corporation Charity School 1811'.

Charity schools were a vital part of education in England in the eighteenth and nineteenth centuries. They were funded by wealthy people who wanted to help the poor receive an education. As blue was the colour traditionally associated with charity, many of these charity schools provided a distinctive blue uniform for its pupils and led to them being known as 'Blue Coat Schools'. The statues in the niches of the Corporation Charity School wear the frock coat and stockings that was the standard uniform for these schools.

The school remained in service until 1923. After it closed the Blue Coat Corporation Charity School Foundation continued to do good work in education. The school building was remodelled when the pupils left and has been used for retail purposes ever since.

Above left: Northampton's charitable residents helped to educate the poor and needy.

Above right: A statue on the Corporation Charity School depicts the pupil's uniform.

19. Northampton Cathedral (1825)

The Cathedral Church of Our Lady Immaculate and St Thomas of Canterbury stands on Barrack Road and is at the heart of the Catholic community in Northampton.

Henry VIII established the Church of England in the sixteenth century and consequently, throughout the seventeenth and eighteenth centuries, Catholics and their associated ceremonies were outlawed. When Northampton gradually became a town strongly associated with the Puritans, a strict Protestant movement that had a desire to 'purify' Christianity of all its grand rituals and have a simpler form of worship, all remaining Catholics left. It was only after an Act of Parliament in 1791 that Catholics were allowed to practise again.

Father William Foley came to Northampton in 1825 to find a site for a new Catholic church. Funds were tight, but a plot of land was purchased on the site of a ruined priory. A small chapel, dedicated to St Andrew, was subsequently built using stone from the original priory, which had also been dedicated to St Andrew. In 1844, Augustus Welby Northmore Pugin was hired to extend this small chapel and he built a large extension to it.

Pugin was an important figure in ecclesiastical architecture and a leader in the Gothic Revival movement. He stated that modern Christian architecture should follow the building traditions of the medieval age, which Pugin believed was a better time. His work has the characteristic, pointed style of medieval Gothic churches. Pugin also created some major secular structures: both the interior of the Houses of Parliament and the tower that houses Big Ben are to his design.

Above: Northampton Cathedral has some exceptional stained-glass work.

Left: Northampton Cathedral developed from a small chapel.

Pugin further expanded the church in Northampton into a cathedral. His design needed to be both inexpensive and fast to produce, so he used local red brick, which was a controversial choice, but it was much quicker to work with than stone and a lot cheaper. Pugin died before completion but his son finished the build.

Unfortunately, the foundations of Pugin's work started to collapse and the unstable parts of the cathedral had to be replaced. The tower and transepts that stand now are the work of architect Albert Herbert. Although these do not follow Pugin's ideal of pointed Gothic architecture, the simplistic Early English styling is captivating.

Northampton Cathedral still displays Pugin's legacy in the interior. The high, broad nave is lined with white columns whose capitals depict realistic foliage, and the tilework and painted ornamentation are a colourful representation of Pugin's ideal of the neo-Gothic style. The stained glass was commissioned through Hardmans, the leading manufacturer of ecclesiastical glass in the world, who worked closely with Pugin. There are notable religious artworks inside including an impressive carved triptych and a window created by modern stained-glass maker Joseph Nuttgens.

20. St Andrew's Hospital (1838)

St Andrew's Hospital stands on Billing Road. It is a specialist centre for mental health and has been since its design and construction by architect George Wallett in 1838. Despite the hospital being originally known as the Northampton General Lunatic Asylum, it was one of the first compassionate and therapeutic mental health institutions to be created.

The first institution for those suffering with mental health disorders was the infamous Bethlem Asylum in London. This opened at the beginning of the fifteenth century and for 400 unenlightened years it, and similar premises, were run as commercial enterprises where anyone with mental health problems were locked away from society and the asylum owners received a fee. The conditions were appalling and they were a prison rather than a hospital. It was only after an Act of Parliament in 1774 that these asylums became licenced and regularly inspected. Although conditions began to improve, it was slowly and only slightly. The first dedicated mental health hospital was The Retreat in York in the early nineteenth century, where the residents were no longer seen as inmates but patients and they received treatment accordingly.

When Northampton's St Andrew's Hospital was opened in 1838, the first doctor was called Thomas Pritchard, a pioneer in 'moral management'. This method of

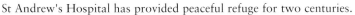

St Andrew's Hospital has provided peaceful refuge for two centuries.

treatment focussed on talking therapies and involving patients in sport, while also teaching work and life skills to prepare them for their eventual release.

St Andrew's remains a leading mental care centre and it is run as a private charity, having chosen not to join the National Health Service.

The building itself is Grade II listed and is classically simple to look at. Its design is symmetrical with three storey, stone walls and a Welsh slate roof. Its symmetry is set off by a central Roman Doric portico, whose semicircular window light has an intricate fan motif.

The hospital chapel also has Grade II listed status and was built in 1863 to a design by Sir George Gilbert Scott. The ironstone walls are highlighted by two-tone brick decorations and the small-scale tower is topped with a suitably minimalistic spire.

21. St Thomas à Becket's Well (1843)

This site on Northampton's Bedford Road has always been a town well. In medieval times it was situated just beyond the town walls and it was here, so folklore has it, that St Thomas à Becket stopped to drink as he fled for his life to France.

Thomas à Becket became Archbishop of Canterbury in the twelfth century and initially had a good relationship with Henry II. However, when Becket began to

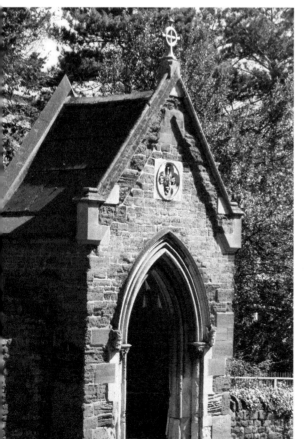

Above: The well's glazed tiles portray the martyrdom of St Thomas.

Left: St Thomas à Becket's Well resembles a shrine.

put the good of the Church before the wealth of the monarchy the relationship soured. Henry brought Becket to be tried for treason at Northampton, the site of the king's court, where Becket was found guilty. Becket had many powerful supporters who facilitated his escape from custody and got him to France. As he was smuggled out of Northampton and down to the river, he stopped at the well to drink. Six years later Thomas à Becket attempted to return to England and his beloved Canterbury Cathedral but the king had Becket assassinated in the cathedral after famously asking, 'Who will free me of the troublesome priest'. Becket's support of Christianity and the Church against the king, and his willingness to die for it, made him a martyr among Christians and he was canonised by the pope soon after his death.

The well from which St Thomas drank subsequently became a site of pilgrimage during medieval times and has been known as St Thomas's well since the thirteenth century.

In 1843 the well was enclosed and covered by the Grade II listed stone shelter that stands there today. The pointed arch and Celtic cross finial combine to make the structure resemble a chapel, as befitting a former site of pilgrimage. However, in the 1950s the well was sealed over and became the site of a bus shelter. The structure was fully restored during the 1980s and the tiled interior depicting two lions was added. It now resembles a grotto and this adds to the interest of this site of historical significance.

22. County Hall (1845)

Although George Row was built in the early eighteenth century, County Hall dates from the mid-nineteenth century when Northampton council commissioned Scottish architect James Milne to design the building. The front alterations were completed in 1900 by property designer Aston Webb, whose work included the Victoria and Albert Museum in London and a redesign of the façade of Buckingham Palace. The building is Grade II listed.

The stone building is comprised of two storeys. The lower floor displays simple square Tuscan pilasters and the arched windows have smooth stone blocking as decoration. The upper level is more elaborate. It has Ionic columns and the relief panels below the roof feature ornate swags.

Although it is called County Hall, the building is only occasionally used by the council. A new modern council office building has been completed just behind County Hall, on Angel Square, and this is where most council business takes place.

The first blue print for a new council building to replace County Hall, which was too small, was proposed in 1973. The design was for a pyramid. It was an open-plan structure, which was state of the art in corporate architecture at that time. The plan was modernist, largely clad in glass and was to be on a hill on the outskirts

Above: County Hall was a Victorian rebuild of an eighteenth-century terrace.

Left: County Hall has elaborately sculpted stone decorations.

The modern Angel Square building now houses the council offices.

of Northampton. The plan was never realised, however, as council finances came under pressure and there were more important things to spend the budget on.

New county council offices were eventually built in Angel Square. The design has a glass façade, as did the futuristic pyramid from 1973, and features copper finials that take their inspiration from tooling used in the local shoemaking industry. The interior is open and airy and allows all areas of the offices to be seen from anywhere else within the building. The project ran into financial difficulties and the council had to sell the office block to raise the necessary funds to complete it. They now lease it from the purchaser. The Victorian County Hall is still owned by the council. As Angel Square was designed without a council chamber, the local authority uses the original one in the George Row property, which dates from 1845.

23. The Parade (former Corn Exchange) (1851)

Situated on the Market Square, this magnificent neoclassical structure was constructed in 1851 as a site for agricultural trade. The suitably grand building was attended by gentleman farmers, who accessed it through the exterior steps that lead to its three arched doorways. The four-storey property was designed by

Decorative columns add architectural interest to the former Corn Exchange.

local architects Alexander and Hull, who used Ionic columns on its façade to give the impression of added height.

The Grade II listed Corn Exchange was also used as a venue for town meetings and dances and a pipe organ was fitted in the 1890s to improve the facilities for entertainments. Travelling film shows began to use the venue and, as the farmers meetings decreased, the Corn Exchange gradually began to host purely leisure activities. The building was converted to a cinema in 1924 and called The Exchange. The Exchange was the first cinema in the country, outside of London, to show 'talkies', and it screened *The Jazz Singer* in 1929 to mass audiences. When the cinema was taken over by the Odeon company in the 1960s it began to fall out of use and eventually became a bingo hall before being restored. It is now a popular bar called The Parade.

24. Clare Street Drill Hall (1859)

Clare Street Drill Hall has a Grade II listing as it is an important piece of military architecture. It was commissioned for the army in 1859 and used by the First Northamptonshire Rifle Volunteer Corps for many years. It is still in use by the military as a centre for the Army Reserve, who are also volunteers.

The building on the site was designed to be a store for militia equipment, with residential accommodation for a commissioned sergeant, who led the troop, and a small military hospital. The large yard was used by the volunteers to practise their drills. The barrel-ceilinged drill hall was added a few years later to protect the volunteers from inclement weather.

The architectural design is fortified Gothic Revival and this style was used to garner local pride and attract recruits. The whole frontage originally had crenelated parapets and in Victorian times the building appeared strikingly similar to the gatehouse at Windsor Castle. These crenelations have since been removed, leaving the parapet unadorned, apart from a cornice running around the roofline. The drill hall is built in red brick with a slate roof and is symmetrical. The stone facings add decoration to its windows and doors. The property is set back from the road and has an imposing air, with two unarmed cannon positioned outside behind cast-iron railings. The drill hall has recently undergone major refurbishments to ensure it serves the local military volunteers for the years to come.

Above: Clare Street Drill Hall protected military volunteers from bad weather.

Right: Cannon still represent military pride outside Clare Street Drill Hall.

25. Beckett and Sargeant's School (1862)

Beckett and Sargeant's School is a Grade II listed property on Kingswell Street. This attractive Gothic Revival building was designed and built in 1862 by Northampton architect Edmund Francis Law. It is built in red brick with both stone and ironstone decorations surrounding the windows and doorway, and stone columns are a feature of the arched, traceried windows on both storeys. Inscribed tiling runs just below the roofline, spelling out the school's name and the date of its original founding, 1735.

The School for Girls was initially set up by two Northampton ladies: Mrs Beckett and her sister Miss Sargeant. The two wealthy philanthropists used their own income to found the school, which started in 1735 and taught thirty poor and needy girls. Their curriculum included religious education, housecraft and needlework. The stone figure above the door of the school represents a pupil in the eighteenth century, complete with a piece of needlework for which the school was noted.

Beckett and Sargeant's School is an attractive red-brick property.

Above left: Beckett and Sargeant pupils learned needlecraft to an excellent standard.

Above right: The statue of Charles II was festooned with oak apples.

The Beckett and Sargeant schoolgirls were also involved with a seventeenth-century tradition that continues to this day in Northampton. 'Oak Apple Day' is observed annually on 29 May. It commemorates the restoration of the monarchy, the day Charles II was returned to the throne after the rule of Oliver Cromwell. On Oak Apple Day it was traditional to wear a sprig of oak apple to show loyalty to the crown. The people of Northampton were immensely thankful and loyal to the king for his direct financial help in rebuilding Northampton after the Great Fire. A service was held each Oak Apple Day in respect of this and the statue of Charles II in All Saints Church was crowned with a wreath. The Beckett and Sargeant pupils were chosen to complete this ceremony and wore a garland of oak apples over their distinctive school uniform as they did so. Although the school has been closed for some years, the laying of the wreath still continues, one of the few places in the country where the traditions of Oak Apple Day are still remembered.

After the school closed, the building continued to be used for the benefit of the young as it became a Youth Advisory Centre. The Beckett and Sargeant Foundation still exists, however. It is a charitable fund helping school pupils in need in wider Northamptonshire.

26. College Street Chapel (1863)

This Grade II listed ecclesiastical building was designed and built by William Hall in 1863. It stands on College Street and is now known as the New Testament Church of God. When it was built it was one of the first nonconformist churches in Northampton and called College Street Baptist Chapel.

Despite being a Victorian building, the architecture has an unmistakeably Georgian influence, with the impressive portico resting on six Corinthian pillars. Three doorways are sheltered beneath this canopy with access straight from the street. It has a massive neoclassical façade that is constructed of smooth stone blocks, while the rear and sides of the building are built of unfaced stone.

The magnificent classical façade of College Street Baptist chapel.

The New Testament Church of God, a branch of the Baptist movement, has worshipped in the building for over half a century and it remains a lively and well-attended chapel. It is also a distinctive and impressive structure on a quiet Northampton street.

27. Guildhall (1864)

The Guildhall is an impressive building that dominates St Giles Square. As Northampton's town hall, it is the base of the borough council and is also used for weddings and exhibitions. The building was commissioned in 1861, when the old town hall on the site became too small. The architect to win the contract was Edward William Godwin, who was just twenty-eight years old at the time and a controversial choice. The new Guildhall was opened to much acclaim with a lavish ceremony in 1864.

The building has an attractive neo-Gothic design in brown and grey stone. The clock tower, which was essentially fashionable to the Victorians, is set into a Welsh slate roof. A modern extension was added in 1992 and was planned to be sympathetic to the original Godwin design. It complements the older part of the building perfectly.

Fourteen statues of British monarchs and saints decorate the property. Each has its own niche and is flanked on either side by windows. The porchway leads to the main entrance, where two friezes celebrate Danish influence in Northampton.

Right: Northampton Guildhall is a focal point of the town.

Below: The late twentieth-century extension fits seamlessly with the original Guildhall.

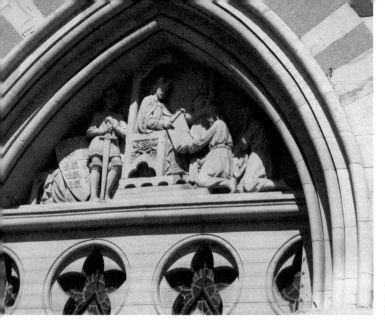

A frieze on the Guildhall shows the founding of Northampton.

The first frieze pictures the invasion of Great Britain by Danish longships. This occurred in the ninth century and the Danish went on to found the town of Northampton. The second frieze was a tribute to the future bride of Edward VII, Princess Alexandra of Denmark. The tableaux were both opened by the princess on a visit to the town.

The interior of the Guildhall is no less magnificent than its exterior. There is fine painted decoration throughout and many works of art. The Great Hall is decorated with large murals of heroes with links to Northampton. It was produced in 1925 by the famous mural artist Colin Unwin Gill.

28. No. 1 Victoria Gardens (1875)

This house is an unexpected find on the corner of Victoria Gardens. Its visual appearance seems completely out of context to its setting, but as it was originally used as commercial premises, this explains its eye-catching design.

Built in 1875, at the same time as the other properties on the street, the mock-Swiss chalet look was a ploy to bring customers to No. 1, which was then a grocery store. The black and white design attracted Edwardian tourists, curious about its unique appearance and naturally they wanted to make purchases there. It was also a tea shop for many years but has recently been converted into student accommodation.

The two-storey building has a slate-roofed turret, complete with a weathervane. The roof is finished with ornate fascias and wide eaves overhanging its gable end. Although the property is built completely in red brick, the upper floor is clad in a riot of black and white timbering and has wooden slatted balconies, which are a decorative, rather than functional, element of the casement windows. Due to its architectural curiosity value, No. 1 Victoria Gardens is listed Grade II by Historic England.

No. 1 Victoria Gardens
was built to resemble a
Swiss chalet.

The turret on
No. 1 Victoria
Gardens is of
architectural merit.

29. Crockett and Jones Shoe Factory (1879)

Northampton's Crockett and Jones shoe company are a successful producer of high-quality footwear and have been trading for over 140 years. The company has always been on Perry Street and their factory is still owned by the fifth generation of the same family.

Brothers-in-law James Crockett and Charles Jones set up the factory in 1879, thanks to a grant from the Thomas White Trust. This local trust enabled 'young men of Northampton the chance to set up a business of their own'. The two men were given £100 each and they began to produce shoes for ladies and gentlemen with their team of twenty workers.

As trade and the workforce grew, the factory expanded until it was one of the largest industrial sites in Northampton. The factory had major extensions built in 1910 and the architect used steel framed buildings that were innovative at that time. Further alterations to the factory took place in 1935 and these have left many art deco design features. The side of the building has an art deco doorway with original exterior light fittings.

The red-brick factory has a large proportion of glass. This was to allow in a lot of natural light and enable fine workmanship, but also made working conditions

Crockett and Jones shoes is family owned after five generations.

Above: Crockett and Jones shoes are an exclusive Northampton brand.

Right: The Crockett and Jones factory has stunning art deco features.

uncomfortable. The factory became very hot when the sun shone and very cold during the winter months due to the poor insulation it afforded. The multiple windows all have stone facings to match the stone frieze across the front of the property, which bears the company name. The interior offices retain their original character including wooden door handles worn smooth with use, frosted glass door panels and vintage filing cabinets. The factory is Grade II listed.

Crockett and Jones have produced some notable footwear including boots for the 1914 Shackleton Antarctic mission, and in the James Bond films *Skyfall* and *Spectre*, Crockett and Jones shoes are worn by the hero. During the Second World War the company ceased general production to make over a million pairs of boots for the British military. The exclusive brand is still in high demand.

30. Albion Brewery (1884)

The Albion Brewery on Kingswell Street is a microbrewery and bar. It is run by the relaunched Northampton brand the Phipps Brewing Company. The brewery stands above a wellhead, called the King's Well, and this is the water used to brew the beers. It has stood on the site since 1884.

The building is one of just a few surviving Victorian tower breweries in the country. The red-brick building is several storeys tall and this height originally

Above: Albion Brewery made power by cascading water from roof tanks.

Left: Albion Brewery customers can see the brewing process on-site.

powered the brewing machinery using the force of water falling from tanks in the roof space. This method proved far more economical than using steam engines.

The property was built by the Northampton brewers Ratliffe and Jeffrey, but they were soon bought out by the Phipps Company. Phipps NBC (Northampton's Brewing Company) was founded in the town in 1801 and were very successful. They remained an independent brewery and changed sites many times, but in 1960 they were finally taken over by Watney Mann and then by Carlsberg Tetley. At this point the brand disappeared.

The Albion Brewery building was used for beer making until 1919 when Phipps production became too large for the site and they moved on. The building and equipment were then used to make lemonade, and in 1954 the building changed use completely and became a tannery, producing the leather covers used by Filofax.

In 2014, the Phipps brand relaunched and now brewing occurs again in the original Albion Brewery building. Customers in the bar can observe beer production through a glass screen between them and the equipment. The Kings Well is still sourced in the cellar. The bar also has a medieval malt oven on display. The oven, dating from the thirteenth century, was discovered during excavations of a nearby archaeological site and it forms a suitable link between the brewing heritage of Northampton and modern beer making.

31. Museum and Art Gallery (1884)

The building housing Northampton Museum and Art Gallery stands on Guildhall Road. It consists of two wings: the original block of 1884 and a brand-new glass extension opened in 2019. They have very different architectural styles and contain the most extensive collection of shoes in the world.

With its heritage of shoemaking, it is not surprising that Northampton Museum has dedicated the whole of its ground floor to the history of shoes and other footwear. It owns over 12,000 pairs and the collection has continued to grow since the museum was first founded in 1870. The oldest pairs exhibited come from ancient Egypt and the rest of the collection explores both the uses and fashions of footwear.

The museum came to the Guildhall Road site soon after the building was constructed in 1884. As the building was also used by the town library at that time, display space was limited. When the library found new premises in 1910, the museum could expand and begin to fully exhibit its internationally important shoe display.

The museum is built of red brick and set with tall, stone-faced windows to let in natural light. The roof apex is arched and this creates a bright and welcoming exhibition hall. The new extension fits seamlessly with the original building as it is also constructed of red brick and heavily glazed. The extension has provided better access to the museum and new facilities for visitors.

Above: Northampton Museum has both Victorian and modern architectural styles.

Left: Northampton Museum has the largest shoe collection in the world.

32. Royal and Derngate Theatre (1884)

The Royal and Derngate Theatre was created in 2006 when the Theatre Royal and the Derngate Theatre combined. The two were originally separate venues, the Royal on Guildhall Road and the Derngate on a site behind it. A £14 million refit taking eighteen months was needed to complete the amalgamation.

The Royal had been built as the Opera House in 1884, by well-known theatre architect C. J. Phipps. In 1927, when the theatre became the base of the Northampton Repertory Players, the name was changed to the Theatre Royal. The repertory company are still at the theatre and produce at least six of their original works every year. In the 1930s Errol Flynn, who was to become one of the most famous film stars of his generation, was a member of the Rep and a film room has been named after him.

The entrance to the Royal is a small stuccoed entrance of three classical arches. This leads to a large tiered auditorium seating an audience of 450. The theatre has Grade II listed status for its interior. It still has many of its original Victorian features including elaborate columns used to support the balconies and private boxes. The large ceiling dome has elegantly painted plasterwork and this decoration continues down to the stage. The safety curtain is of note. It was presented to the Royal by its creator, Henry Bird, in 1978. Bird was a local artist

The Royal and Derngate complex is a versatile entertainment space.

Above: The
Royal Theatre
retains its elegant
nineteenth-century
interior.

Left: A brutalist
architectural style
was used for the
Derngate Theatre.

who went on to become renowned for his set designs countrywide. The safety curtain is a wonderful example of his painting.

Northampton Borough Council commissioned the Derngate Theatre in 1983. The architects behind it, Renton, Howard, Wood and Lewin, designed other famous modern theatres including Sadler's Wells in London and the Crucible in Sheffield. It is a large open plan building, and will seat 1,200 people who can experience anything from snooker to classical concerts. It was purposely designed to be a flexible and adaptable space. The more formal layout of the Royal is better suited for stage productions.

The 2013 addition of the Errol Flynn Filmhouse gives even more versatility to the complex as films can now be screened. All entertainment modes and audiences are catered for within the theatres and their vastly contrasting architectural styles.

33. The Bear (c. 1890)

The Bear, on Sheep Street, is a typical example of a traditional nineteenth-century pub. It has been built in mock-Tudor style, with a black and white painted front and bay windows with leaded lights. The Bear is on the site of a much older structure and the historically interesting remains of this building can be seen in the pub's cellar.

In the twelfth century Northampton was one of the most important and affluent towns in England because it was the seat of the king's court. Like most large towns at that time, it had a large Jewish population and the community was centred in the area around Sheep Street. Despite periods of exile, the Jewish community in Northampton still flourished and by medieval times there had constructed many large stone buildings. One of these was the synagogue.

The Bear is on the site of the ancient synagogue.

It is known that the synagogue survived the Great Fire of Northampton and was still being shown on town maps as late as the eighteenth century. Subsequent redevelopment has altered Sheep Street completely and no trace of the synagogue can now be seen above ground; however, the cellar walls and an internal staircase do still exist. The cellar of The Bear now incorporates these important archaeological remains. It occupies the synagogue site, the heart of the Jewish community for nearly a thousand years.

34. St Matthew's Church (1893)

The Church of St Matthew was consecrated in 1893 in memory of Pickering Phipps. It has a commanding corner position and also contains some incredible pieces of modern art.

Pickering Phipps was an important man in Northampton. He was not only the owner of the local Phipps brewery, but also mayor of Northampton in

St Matthew's Church has an attractive corner position.

the 1860s, an MP in the 1870s and a philanthropist. He had provided land in the Kingsley Park area, where St Matthew's stands, to create a new housing estate for the Northampton residents. A temporary iron church had been erected in the 1880s for the new estate, but Phipps had always planned to fund a proper place of worship. He died before he could fulfil this wish but his family commissioned local architect Matthew Henry Holding to design St Matthew's Church in his memory.

The design for the church was Victorian Gothic style. It was imposingly built using small bricks of local stone and it had buttresses as a design feature. The slate roof and tower are finished with a small spire.

The first vicar was Canon Rowden Hussey. He was succeeded as vicar by his son, Walter, who was responsible for sourcing the works of art in St Matthew's. Walter Hussey was a patron of the arts and in particular modern artists. He commissioned Henry Moore to produce a stone sculpture, the *Madonna and Child*, in 1944, which he did at very little cost. This is displayed near the lady chapel in St Matthew's. It has, on occasion, been on loan to museums and exhibitions as it is an important example of Moore's work. In 1946 he persuaded Graham Sutherland to create the painting *The Crucifixion* especially for the

Stone buttresses are an architectural design feature on St Matthew's.

St Matthew's contains
art by Henry Moore
and Graham Sutherland.

church. The painting is oil on board that, in the austere years after the Second World War, was an inexpensive method of production. Hussey also got composer Benjamin Britten to write music for the church choir. A more recent artwork is a life-size bronze of St Matthew. It was made in 2009 by Ian Rank-Broadly, who is an eminent contemporary sculptor responsible for producing the model for the Queen's Head, which is used on recently minted coins.

The church stands on Kettering Road, just above the racecourse, and it has a Grade II listing as it is an important piece of Victorian architecture.

35. City Building (1900)

The building that stands on the corner of Fish Street is a Grade II listed example of art nouveau commercial property design. This building, known as the City Building, was designed by architect Alexander Anderson in the late nineteenth century as warehousing for Malcolm Inglis & Co., a successful leather and hide importer.

Alexander Anderson was born in Glasgow and studied at the Glasgow School of Art and Design and Malcom Inglis & Co. were a Glaswegian company who had begun trading in the eighteenth century. The man who brought the two to Northampton was councillor David Taylor. Taylor was also Glasgow born, a director of Malcolm Inglis & Co. and a friend of Alexander Anderson. Councillor Taylor suggested the leather company move to the shoemaking heart of Great Britain and then engaged Anderson to design the buildings for them.

For a commercial property, the building has surprisingly decorative features, but these are typical of the art nouveau style of the architect. A pair of carved bulls heads on pilasters are a striking feature and the lettering and garlands decorating the frieze bearing the company name are a good example of art nouveau design.

The door canopy features sculpting by the leading stone mason of his generation, Abraham Broadbent.

The City Building has changed occupier over time. It was used by the local council as offices and has now been converted for use as accommodation and retail units. The building was used in the 1970s as a location for filming the television series *Doctor Who*. The interior became a set for the story 'The Talons of Weng-Chiang'. Two other Northampton locations were used in the BBC production: the Royal Theatre and St Crispin's Hospital.

The City Building was warehousing built with art nouveau styling.

Decorative bulls' heads show the occupier was a leather supplier.

The City Building's door frieze was by a leading sculptor.

36. Central Library (1910)

The Central Library is an elegant, stone-fronted building and was created by local architect Herbert Norman. The design reflects a much earlier classical style of architecture, with statues decorating the façade in bespoke niches and a stone balustrade. It has Grade II listed status.

Attitudes in the middle of the nineteenth century favoured enlightening people to classical literature, believing that this would improve standards of behaviour. After a Northampton MP stated that a library would be 'a good step towards redeeming the moral character of the town,' a lending library was incorporated into the Guildhall museum. It included a reference library and a reading room with shelves stocked with 12,000 volumes. This proved too small and a new separate building for the library was proposed. Philanthropist Andrew Carnegie provided the funds for it.

Andrew Carnegie was an American rail magnate and the richest man in the world at that time. He had been born in Great Britain in 1835, but when his family suffered economic hardship they moved to the United States. The young Carnegie got a job on the railways where hard work and integrity led to promotion. He invested his income back into the railroad and grew to be a powerful businessman. In later life Carnegie used his wealth to help others in both America and Great Britain. He had a particular passion for providing the funding for libraries. Northampton has one of the 3,000 libraries Carnegie funded wordwide, and it stands as a testament to his generosity.

The site for the library was to be Abington Street and construction was completed in 1910. It has two storeys above ground and a basement, all linked with an eye-catching marble staircase. The library is still true to its purpose of education for all and, while the library service has been updated to provide modern and efficient technology, the building has kept much of its original appearance with the Edwardian plasterwork and glass. The library has the dignified atmosphere of a place where Northampton residents can take time out to explore literature.

Northampton Central Library has a neoclassical stone façade with statues.

Free access to literature was believed to improve behavioural standards.

37. Northampton School for Boys (1911)

Northampton School for Boys was originally founded in 1541 and called Northampton Town and County Grammar School. It remained in an adapted church building in Northampton town centre for over 300 years until the premises were no longer safe and a new site was needed. Despite a brief move to Abington Square in 1870, it became apparent that only a purposely designed new school would be suitable. This is the school building that now stands on Billing Road. It was completed in 1911 and changed its name to Northampton Grammar School for Boys.

Contrary to its name, the school accepts female pupils for sixth form study, as well as boys from the ages of eleven to eighteen. It is one of the best learning establishments in the county and constantly oversubscribed. This prestige is reflected by the school motto: 'A Tradition of Excellence'. Tradition also plays a part in day-to-day school life; it has a house system with prefects and puts emphasis on excelling in extracurricular activities, especially music and sports. Past pupils include the actor Matt Smith, Nobel Prize winner Francis Crick and software engineer Bear Morten.

Above: Northampton School for Boys has many well-known former pupils.

Below: Northampton School for Boys' motto is 'A Tradition of Excellence'.

The school has two main blocks, one being the original 1911 build and another modern block, which followed nearly a century later, in 2007. The older part of the school commands a wide plot, set back from the roadside. It is constructed in red brick with stone decorations and has plenty of sash windows to let in natural light. The tall chimney stacks and a small bell tower both give the building height. The front of the school bears the title 'Northampton Grammar School', and also depicts the school crest in the form of two heraldic shields. One shield has two lions and the motto '*Castello Fortior Concordia*', which means 'Peace is stronger than a fortress', and the other bears the Northampton insignia and the motto '*Rosa Concordiae Signum*', which means 'A rose, a symbol of peace'. The importance of peace was vital in the sixteenth century when the school was founded, as England was often in conflict with other European countries.

The new part of the building won awards for design from the Royal Institute of British Architects. The block is ecologically efficient and sustainable construction materials have been used. Although the design is uber modern, the new block perfectly complements the older building, drawing on the linear red brick and stone decoration of the 1911 design. The school can now house 450 extra pupils in seventeen new classrooms.

38. Barratts Shoe Factory (1913)

The large, elaborately styled, neo-baroque shoe factory that stands on Kingsthorpe Road was commissioned by the Barratts shoe company. It is a Grade II listed building, built of both stone and brick and also has details picked out in terracotta. The roof balustrade announces the words 'Footshape' and 'Bootworks', leaving no doubt as to the purpose of the factory. The main door is flanked with Ionic columns and a clock sits centrally above it. The size and grandeur of this industrial building is evidence of how important shoemaking was, and still is, to Northampton.

The medieval term for a shoemaker was a 'cordwainer', and Northampton was a logical site for the cordwaining trade to develop in the Middle Ages. The good soil in the area grew excellent hay and this in turn established a strong cattle farming community. The nearby River Nene and oak forests provided both the water and oak bark needed to tan the hides of the cattle locally, and leather became readily available. The central position of Northampton on a good road system allowed the cordwainers the opportunity to transport their wares and they thrived, until by Victorian times there were nearly 2,000 shoemakers in the town. Northampton footwear had a strong reputation and was the first choice for the military when they commissioned 4,000 pairs of boots in 1642. The shoe producers of Northampton worked together to complete this order and it secured their status as the best and most reliable in the country.

Literacy skills in the working-class population of Northampton was unusually high until the nineteenth century, due to the need for shoemakers to work with precise

Above: Barratt's elaborate factory reflected the high quality of their shoes.

Below: After factories were built, shoemaking stopped being a cottage industry.

Barratts Shoes were a successful business for a hundred years.

measurements and sizing and be able to write everything down. Many worked from their homes in cottage industries until, in 1861, the first steam-powered machinery arrived. The industry moved from a domestic setting to large factories and the age of mass production in Northampton began.

Doc Marten boots and Stylo Matchmaker football boots were both manufactured in the town and Barratts owned both of these brands from the 1960s. Therefore, it was the Barratts factory on Kingsthorpe Road that were responsible for producing these iconic boots of the 1970s.

Barratts built their ornate factory in 1913 and this lavish style was echoed in the colourful, glossy brochures the company produced in the 1920s and '30s to promote their products to the fashionable middle class. Barratts became a popular high street brand and were a success for a hundred years. Unfortunately, the economic pressures of the twenty-first century proved too much and the company finally went into receivership in 2013, exactly a century after the Kingsthorpe Road factory had first opened.

39. No. 78 Derngate (1916)

Derngate is the only street in Northampton that is still called by its original name. Derngate comes from the ancient term 'Darngate', which means 'route to the river', and indeed the properties on Derngate enjoy clear views of the nearby River Nene from their back gardens.

No. 78 Derngate is a Grade II listed terraced house built of red brick with a welsh slate roof, and although it was originally constructed in 1815, it is best known for the complete remodelling of its interior by Charles Rennie Mackintosh during the years of the First World War.

This is the only design that Mackintosh produced outside of Scotland and was one of his final major works. He died in 1928 at the age of seventy. The Derngate house was commissioned by his patron, Northampton businessman Wenman

Above: Charles Rennie Mackintosh's interior at No. 78 Derngate has been restored.

Right: The front door of No. 78 Derngate is iconic Mackintosh design.

The three-storey rear extension influenced the art deco movement.

Joseph Bassett-Lowke, as his first family home. The interior design was years ahead of its time and incorporated central heating, indoor plumbing and labour-saving electrical equipment for the kitchen. The interior decoration is an excellent example of Charles Rennie Mackintosh's trademark design.

Charles Rennie Mackintosh was born in Glasgow in 1868 and as an art student, he followed the art nouveau movement before breaking away to the simpler industrial designs of the modernists. His works are renowned worldwide. Although primarily an architect, he was equally as interested in the details and decoration of his designs. This is evident in No. 78 Derngate where his ceramic fireplaces, wall-mounted lighting and wooden screens are an integral part of the property.

When Bassett-Lowke moved out of the house it was used as classrooms by the Northampton School for Girls before falling into disrepair. In 2002, No. 78 Derngate was restored in its entirety and opened to the public. The restoration was achieved by the renovation of what remained and replicating what had been lost. Mackintosh's colour scheme has been restored and this features the use of monochrome and primary colours. Mackintosh's influence on the later art deco movement can clearly be seen in the exceptional designs that he produced.

40. Memorial Hall (1921)

The memorial hall on Castilian Street was designed in 1919 by architect Alexander Ellis Anderson and completed in 1921 by local firm Henry Martin Ltd. The property was recently listed Grade II as it is an unusual example of an English building constructed in the Scottish Baronial style.

The hall is built of red brick and sandstone and has eye-catching conical roof turrets. The bold inscription above the door declares that it was built to commemorate those who had fallen in the First World War, which is true, but a further inscription, just below the roof line, reveals another memorial.

The inscribed initials 'R.P.T.' denote Ralph Paton Taylor, who was just twenty years old when he was killed at the Battle of the Somme. His father was a local

The Memorial Hall's architecture is more usually seen in Scotland.

The Memorial Hall commemorates the dead of the First World War.

councillor, David Paton Taylor, who funded the Memorial Hall and built it in memory of his son. David Paton Taylor had been born in Scotland, and he asked a fellow scot, Alexander Anderson, to produce an architectural design that drew on their heritage. This explains the unique, traditionally Scottish appearance of the property.

The interior of the Memorial Hall has remained mostly intact. The stone balconies that surround the open-plan great hall survive, as does much of the original stained glass. This includes the crest of the Northampton Regiment in which Ralph Paton Taylor served. The Memorial Hall is now a bar with residential accommodation above.

Prior to the hall being built, the site was occupied by a property called Castilian House, and this was used during the First World War as an auxiliary hospital for the Voluntary Aid Detachment. The new Memorial Hall was also used to help the armed forces when, in the 1920s, it was run by the Young Women's Christian Association as a hostel for war veterans. Their emblem is carved on an entablature inside the hall. It poignantly reads: 'By Love Serve One Another'.

41. New Ways (1926)

New Ways, a Grade II listed house on Wellingborough Road, was commissioned by Wenman Joseph Bassett-Lowke, a Northampton producer of model railways, in 1926. The name of the house is apt, as Bassett-Lowke was a patron of the forward-thinking modernist architects Charles Rennie Mackintosh and the designer of New Ways, the German expressionist Peter Behrens.

The property was built with many new features never before seen in an English building. It had a flat roof, central heating in every room and featured a stunning

Above: New Ways was designed by modernist architect Peter Behrens.

Right: New Ways was built with innovative features.

art deco interior. Bassett-Lowke previously lived at No. 78 Derngate, designed by Mackintosh, and New Ways contains some of the original wall features and furniture from the house. These originals have been used to make accurate reproductions for the restored Derngate property.

New Ways is a simple whitewashed cement home. It is built in perfect symmetry, with striking features. These include the decorative central window at the front, the lack of upper windows and a balconied rear elevation with patio doors. Steel rods project from the flat roof and give the impression of battlements, perhaps in appreciation of Bassett-Lowke's often quoted belief that 'an Englishman's home is his castle'. Bassett-Lowke lived here until his death, when New Ways was sold and is now privately owned.

42. Racecourse Pavilion (1930)

Northampton Racecourse is on Kettering Road and its pavilion is a stylish, white, art deco building. The Pavilion has had a commanding view of the activities in the area since the original Victorian grandstand was altered to create it in 1930. Unlike the grandstand, the Pavilion has never been used to view horseracing. Racing was officially stopped on the racecourse at the turn of the twentieth century due to fatalities that had occurred. Despite this, the Grade II listed building is an impressive part in the long history of the site.

The first race meetings, without an official track, took place in the seventeenth century. In 1727 a properly constructed course was laid out with financial help from Lord Spencer of nearby Althorp. This anti-clockwise track, which proved to be very challenging for both horses and jockeys, became a popular meet. It was

The art deco Pavilion was reconstructed from the Victorian grandstand.

regularly visited by royalty and an impressive grandstand was constructed in
1844. The course continued to be a challenge and it was proved unsafe after the
death of a spectator in 1904. All racing ceased.

The racecourse always had a variety of uses. In the 1770s the area was renamed
Freeman's Common and used by Northampton residents to graze their animals.
This was entertaining on race days when livestock that found their way onto the
course occasionally ended up racing alongside the horses and were sometimes bet
on to win! In the First World War the racecourse was used as a training base for
16,000 troops and their 7,000 horses. However, by 1917 the ground was needed
to help provide food for the town and it was ploughed and used for allotments.
After the war ended, the racecourse site was converted to playing fields, including
football and cricket pitches, bowling greens and children's recreational areas.

The sportsmen and women at the site needed a venue for afternoon tea, as
was the fashion in the interwar years. The solution was the construction of the
Pavilion in 1930. Although the Victorian grandstand was used as a base, only
the foundations were retained and the Pavilion was designed as a completely
new building.

It is a two-storey stuccoed property built in an Oriental art deco style. The roof
canopy is reminiscent of a pagoda and is supported on elegant cast-iron columns.

Metal detailing on the Pavilion building has an Oriental influence.

An exterior feature is the six-arch arcade on the lower floor, and the first floor has a covered exterior gallery to protect viewers on rainy days. Often known as the Jade Pavilion after a Chinese restaurant that used to occupy it, the Pavilion has hosted many events and is now the site of Northampton's Umbrella Fair, a community and family arts festival held every August.

43. The Jesus Centre (1936)

The cinema building situated on Abington Square is an exceptional piece of art deco design and arguably the best work by cinema architect William Riddell Glen. Glen was architect to Associated British Cinemas and designed many movie theatres of the 1920s and '30s. Glen's designs were usually modernist or art deco in style, but unfortunately most have since been demolished to make way for modern multiplexes. This cinema survived but it suffered. It stood empty and derelict for five years after finally closing due to its unsafe state of repair. It was eventually purchased by the Jesus Fellowship Church and has enjoyed a new lease of life as a Christian centre and entertainment venue.

The white and green building with stunning chrome detailing around the canopy commands a corner site. The front elevation now bears the symbol of the cross, indicating that the property is now a centre of worship for the Jesus Fellowship Church. This church does a lot of social work on the streets and are

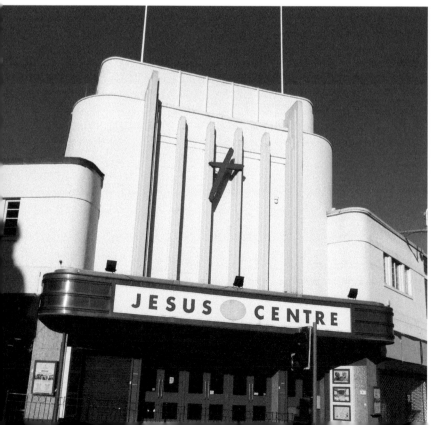

The former 'Savoy' was among the most luxurious of cinemas.

Much of the building's art deco detailing has been preserved.

mainly a young, evangelistic congregation. They prefer to worship in either a domestic or other secular setting, and by purchasing the cinema building, they have allowed this notable piece of architecture to continue to serve the community of Northampton.

Major renovation work has preserved most of the classic art deco interior. The plasterwork around the proscenium arch has a geometric design and has been carefully restored to its original black and white colouring. The door signs are all original and the art deco seat supports in the circle are still in place. English Heritage have supported this venture and ensured that the Grade II listed building has retained most of its stunning art deco features.

The cinema was built in 1936. The Savoy, as it was then called, was heralded as 'Northampton's new super cinema' and 'the last word in comfort'. It had an auditorium large enough for an audience of 2,000 and had sumptuous surroundings and plush seats. In the 1950s the cinema was rebranded as the ABC and it began to host live music performances. The Beatles and The Rolling Stones both played here in the 1960s. The building continued to show mainstream films until it became too costly to repair and closed in 1995.

11. Mounts Baths (1936)

The complex of municipal buildings that stand on Upper Mounts were all built in the 1930s in a statement of civic pride. The group consists of the fire station, police station and local courts but the most outstanding of them is Mounts Baths.

Wenman Joseph Bassett-Lowke, a major advocate of modernist architecture, was chairman of the committee overseeing the construction of the new public buildings and ensured architects J. C Prestwick & Sons won the contract to design the swimming baths with their art deco plans. The Upper Mounts site was an overpopulated section of Northampton but the residents were moved to better conditions in council housing and the old properties demolished to make space for the civic complex. Northampton's old prison had also been in the area; the baths are built on land originally occupied by the prison exercise yard.

Swimming was fashionable in the 1930s for both health and leisure, and when the building opened in 1936, it was with a lavish swimming gala. The Mounts Baths are unusual for a pool built at this time as most pools were outdoor lidos, but the Mounts are entirely indoors. There was always a plan to add an outdoor pool to the baths but this never materialised.

Due to the largely unaltered art deco design, the Mounts Baths are renowned for being one of the most architecturally important swimming pools in the world. The tiered design of the front, with its stone cladding, three doors and the wide entrance steps, give the building a palatial appearance. The side walls of the baths are made glass on a reinforced concrete frame, allowing a lot of natural light into the pool area. The pool hall is supported on eight arches, and these, combined with the overhead natural light, give the pool a church-like appearance.

The baths have constantly been kept in good repair and even following eighty-plus years of use the pool still looks modern and up-to-date. There have been a few changes over the years: the diving boards had to be removed for reasons of health and safety and the plunge pool area has been rebuilt. The hot room, however, is completely original and retains all of its black and white glazing, which the new plunge pool has been designed to match this perfectly. There are two art deco panels in the lobby, originally used to guide the bathers to their correct shower and changing areas, one depicting a female swimmer and the other a male. The tiling in the changing rooms is all original.

The Mounts Baths are part of a municipal buildings complex.

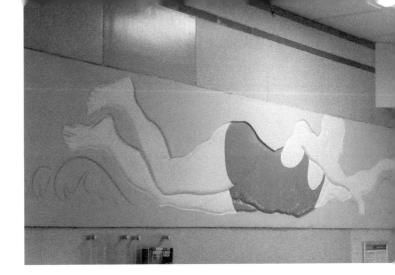

The pool has always promoted the health benefits of swimming.

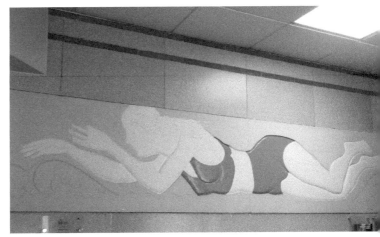

Art deco panels directed bathers to their correct changing rooms.

The Mounts Baths are still as popular today as when they opened. They stand as a testament to the commitment of Northampton council to provide public amenities that promote a healthy lifestyle in the community.

45. Abington Library (1939)

The library on Lindsay Avenue has served the residents of this peaceful interwar housing estate for nearly eighty years. With arched windows, this friendly library has a resemblance to a chapel, which is totally in keeping with the role it has as the hub of the community. The small turret on the roof adds to the chapel-like appearance but is also evidence of the important part of Northampton's history that Abington Library has existed through.

During the Second World War, the little turret on the roof would have held an air-raid siren to sound if enemy aircraft were approaching. The only serious air raid in Northampton occurred in 1941 when the cemetery on Billing Road and the nearby St Andrew's Hospital were bombed. It is believed that the reflection from the marble tombstones was mistaken for blacked-out munitions factory windows. Fortunately, there were no casualties, despite tombstones being blasted through the roofs of nearby housing. Before this attack, not many people used the bomb shelters and ignored air-raid sirens, but after this scare they were much more prudent. An English bomber also crashed in the town. The aircraft got into difficulties and the crew had to eject, leaving the plane heading for a crash landing on open land. However, the aircraft managed to change course at the last minute, entered Northampton town centre and careered down Gold Street before crashing on George Row. Thankfully it was late at night and as the streets were deserted, no one was hurt.

Northampton was not a major site for war industry, although it still continued producing shoes and boots. Most shoemakers switched to making footwear for the armed forces and some companies were tasked with making specialised shoes for secret agents. These came complete with secret compartments and tracking devices. As Northampton was considered a very safe place to be during the Second World War it became home to over 42,000 evacuees from London during the early years of the war.

Northampton Racecourse became a training camp for the armed services for a time. Residents were unhappy to have the racecourse taken out of use as it was the site of many football and cricket pitches, but they supported the war effort and

Abington Library was built just before the Second World War.

Northampton was a safe haven for evacuees during the Blitz.

during the war years most leisure pursuits became confined to the home. The radio was popular, as were board games, but it was reading that provided the most entertainment. Abington lending library was essential to supply the population with books, which it did throughout the Second World War and continues to do so into the twenty-first century.

16. Carlsberg Brewery (1973)

The Carlsberg brewery is in the very heart of Northampton. The large concrete and steel building, with its tall towers and chimneys, has occupied the riverside site for nearly half a century. When it was commissioned in 1973, the factory's brutalist architectural design stood as a symbol for all that was modern and state of the art. The brewery was, and still is, an innovative economic asset to the city.

The brewery sources water from the River Nene and various wells in the vicinity. This area of Northampton has had a brewing industry since the town was first founded. An excavation while building the Carlsberg factory revealed wells, ovens used for malt roasting and wall foundations that proved to be the remains of a large brewery from the thirteenth century. Medieval beer was a much weaker brew than the modern equivalent. It was drunk by everyone, including children, as the fermentation process made it safer to drink than water. Fresh water sources were invariably contaminated by debris from the town's population.

As the water supply became safer, beer drinking became an adult activity and ale was brewed a lot stronger and darker. It was drunk from pottery or leather tankards in large measures and drunkenness became a problem. During the nineteenth century, however, trends changed. A paler, less alcoholic style of beer was brewed in Burton-on-Trent and its popularity spread. This brewing process produced a light, clear beer and to show off its clarity and head, beer was served in glass drinking vessels for the first time.

In 1847, J. C. Jacobsen founded the Carlsberg Brewery in Copenhagen, Denmark, and introduced lager to the drinkers of Great Britain. Lager was similar to the light beer the UK now preferred drinking and Carlsberg soon became the leading lager brand with a major export market. Great Britain was an important consumer for Carlsberg, 'Special Brew' was created for Winston Churchill to commemorate his visit to Denmark in 1950, and the 1958 British film *Ice Cold in Alex* famously features the drinking of Carlsberg lager in its denouement. Initially, no Carlsberg products were made outside of Denmark but the growing market in the UK made this a logical choice for the first expansion site of the Carlsberg industry.

In 1973, plans for a new brewery in Northampton were made and Danish architect Knud Munk was commissioned to undertake the build. His brutalist design, based on an upturned Viking longship, won the Financial Times Industrial Architecture Prize in 1974. Since then Carlsberg, 'Probably the Best Lager in the World' according to its advertising slogan, has continued to bring prosperity to Northampton and its residents.

Carlsberg brewery uses water from the River Nene.

The Carlsberg brewery building won awards for its Danish designer.

47. International Academy (1973)

Northampton International Academy opened in 2018 and it is an outstanding educational facility. It cost £46 million to develop and the site, on Barracks Road, contains as much as a university campus, despite it being contained in a single building. The academy can educate over 2,000 pupils aged from five to nineteen years, and comprises of classrooms, theatres, gyms, sports halls, cafés and other recreational spaces. It is the largest self-contained school of its kind in Great Britain and has been created thanks to the suitability for redevelopment of the original building on the site.

The modern front of the new venture fits seamlessly with the older brutalist structure that has been used to create it. It used to be occupied by the Royal Mail

Northampton International Academy stands on the site of Gibraltar Barracks.

Brutalist architecture was an inexpensive building method but also stylish.

sorting office where, in 1973, planning permission was granted to build it on the site of Gibraltar Barracks. The brutalist architectural style was favoured by both government and corporate bodies at that time as they used concrete. This made the buildings cost effective in terms of materials and building time and the sorting office was completed both quickly and inexpensively. The term brutalist had originated in France in the middle of the twentieth century, where designers such as Corbusier used the building material 'Bèton Brut', which translates as 'raw concrete', to create their modular, modern architecture. The term became corrupted to brutalist in English and the style became functional and unpretentious.

After the Royal Mail moved to another premises, the sorting office stood derelict for many years and a fire in 2003 put the survival of the building in doubt. However, it was considered more cost effective to redevelop the site rather than demolish the concrete building. The massive structure with its large internal spaces was ideal to be converted into the Northampton International Academy, where its 6-metre-high ceilings have allowed for the addition of mezzanines. These contain the many classrooms and surround an immense atrium. The large amount of natural light flooding into the building give an airy and spacious feeling to this pleasant and state-of-the-art learning establishment.

48. The National Lift Tower (1982)

One iconic structure in Northampton is the National lift Tower. It has been affectionately labelled the 'Northampton Lighthouse' and soars to a height of 127 metres. When it was designed and built for the Express Lifts company in 1982, it stood alone, but now it's Weedon Road site is surrounded by a housing development. This has not stopped the tower being a commanding feature on

Above: The National Lift Tower is a well-known Northampton landmark.

Right: The colloquially named 'Northampton Lighthouse' provides vital safety testing.

the Northampton skyline and it has been given a Grade II listing as a 'unique structure'. When this was awarded in 1997, the tower was only fifteen years old and the youngest building to have received listed status.

It was designed by local architect Maurice Walton as a means of testing lift safety. There is only one other testing tower in all of Europe and this is only half the height of the Northampton Lighthouse. The building has a concrete fabrication and was constructed using a process of continuous slip flow. It took over three weeks of constant pouring to complete. The distinctive shaping at the top and the round column of the tower are both design features to reduce wind resistance. Its uniqueness was already recognised when it was opened in 1982 with a ceremony performed by Elizabeth II.

When Express Lifts went out of business in 1997, the tower fell into disuse. Fortunately, in 2009 a private company took over, renovated the structure and it is now still used for safety testing. Inside, there is a high-speed lift shaft that can operate a lift at over 20 miles per hour. When the first ever elevator was installed in a building in New York, it travelled at just half a mile an hour. The Northampton lift is one of the fastest in the world. Some of the 127 metre shafts in the tower are used to test water drainage systems for high-rise buildings and some are used to test safety devices worn by those working at height.

The National Lift Tower has also become a popular venue for charity abseils. Many people have descended from it and it is the tallest permanent abseil tower in the world.

49. *Discovery* (the Francis Crick Memorial) (2005)

Discovery is a sculpture on the main shopping parade in Northampton. The structure, on Abington Street, commemorates the life and achievements of Sir Francis Crick.

Francis Crick, with his friend James Watson, were awarded the Nobel Prize for medicine in 1962 for discovering that the basic code for all life is DNA. The sculpture *Discovery* symbolises that DNA is the most fundamental building material in the universe.

Francis Crick is one of the most famous sons of Northampton. He was born in 1916 in Weston Favell, which is on the outskirts of Northampton. His grandfather was a naturalist and friend of Charles Darwin, so science was an important part of the Crick family life, although his father owned a shoe factory. Francis' grandfather, with an uncle, taught the boy all about science and experiments in a shed at the bottom of the garden, where the preschool Francis was an avid and exceptional pupil.

Crick was later taught at the Northampton School for Boys on Billing Road before going up to study science at University College, London, at a young age. It was here that he met his lifelong friend and co-writer of the paper on DNA

Above left: *Discovery* celebrates the importance of Northampton's scientific revelation.

Above right: Francis Crick did experiments in a Northampton house like this.

James Watson. After graduating the pair specialised in biology research, which finally led to the discovery of DNA. Crick later moved to America, where he lived until his death in 2005. However, his memorial stands in the heart of his home town, Northampton.

The sculpture, *Discovery*, by Lucy Glendinning, is produced in metal and depicts two life-size human figures, each reaching up and twisting to the sky. This is a visual reference to the twist of the double helix of DNA and its importance to human life. It is a striking installation, the focus of Northampton's main shopping street and a testament to the brilliance of Sir Francis Crick.

50. Northgate Bus Station (2014)

Northgate bus station is a modern steel and glass construction on Bradshaw Street. It is light and spacious and replaced the demolished Greyfriars bus station as Northampton's hub of public transport in 2014.

Northampton has had an uneasy relationship with its bus terminals. Problems plagued Northgate bus station on its first day of opening. The town centre was grid-locked all day due to the increased number of buses and the police had to intervene and direct traffic. The bus timetable was subsequently completely revised.

Greyfriars bus station had been voted the third most hated building in Great Britain in a poll completed by *The Guardian,* where it was called 'the mouth of hell' by those familiar with it. The concept of Greyfriars bus station, when it was built in 1976, was innovative. It was built over several floors to provide the much needed space for the increased trade and traffic brought by the newly built Grosvenor Shopping Centre. The top floors were to be office suites and roof gardens for the companies trading in the Grosvenor Centre, the middle floors were additional car parking and the lower floor was given over to the bus station. In actuality, the offices remained empty for most of the time that the building stood and the bus depot proved hard to access by the public. Entry to the complex was provided by underpasses but within two years of them being built, there were stalactites forming on the ceilings due to damp from the ground above. Demolition was a welcome relief for the residents of Northampton.

Archaeological excavations revealed the site for the new bus depot had been the position of the medieval synagogue, which disappeared in the eighteenth century. Much of ancient Northampton has been destroyed. This was either in the Civil War or Northampton's disastrous fire of the seventeenth century. Northgate bus station was named in reflection of its proximity to the ancient entrance to the town. The title is a way to link the heritage of Northampton with its bright future.

Northgate bus station provides a light and spacious environment.

Above: Northgate bus station sits near an ancient place of worship.

Below: The new depot provides a link with old Northampton.

Bibliography

Brown, Cynthia, *Northampton 1835–1985: Shoe Town, New Town* (Chichester: Phillimore & Co. Ltd, 1990)

Stafford, John, *Life in Old Northampton* (Northampton: Belmont Press, 1976)

Thomas, Peter, *Memories of Northampton* (Elland: True North Books Ltd, 1999)

White, A., *The Story of Northampton* (Wakefield: Chantry Press, 1986)